Dear Young Friends

Pope Francis in Conversation with Young People

Dear Young Friends

Pope Francis in Conversation with Young People

Bishop Brendan Leahy

VERITAS

Published 2017 by Veritas Publications
7–8 Lower Abbey Street
Dublin 1, Ireland
publications@veritas.ie
www.veritas.ie

ISBN 978 1 84730 775 0

10 9 8 7 6 5 4 3 2 1

A catalogue record for this book is available from the British Library.

Cover designed by Heather Costello, Veritas Publications
Printed in the Republic of Ireland by KC Print, Killarney, Co. Kerry

*Veritas books are printed on paper made from the wood pulp of managed forests.
For every tree felled, at least one tree is planted, thereby renewing natural
resources.*

Contents

Preface

Pope Francis enjoys meeting young people. He listens carefully to them and chats easily with them. We've all seen images of him with groups of youths stopping for a selfie when asked. As well as talking with young people, he often speaks of them, reminding others how easily they can be forgotten or pushed to the margins of society. He knows only too well that there are forces at work in today's world that want to rob young people of their true freedom and hope, blocking the development of their true personality.

It's no surprise that so many young people, also in Ireland, feel a friendship with the Pope. Somehow, his smiling face reassures and gives hope while, at the same time, his words and example give direction. Together with thousands from Ireland, I witnessed Pope Francis engage with over a million young adults from all corners of the world at the World Youth Day in Kraków in July 2016. It was an amazing experience. Those who had been at previous World Youth Days said there was something special about the way he communicated – his message was so clear, understandable and penetrating.

In his simple way of speaking, Pope Francis has a powerful message. He is not into offering simplistic answers to life's challenges, nor the pursuit of fashionable trends. He puts before young people the deep questions they themselves ask and he enters into a dialogue with them, sharing his own life experience, communicating a wisdom he has distilled from the ups and downs of life. He too admits that he finds some of life's questions perplexing and mysterious.

He is keen to help young people find the courage to take the important steps that need to be taken when they are young. Important choices are made in youth. Life directions can be established. If there is one point Pope Francis keeps coming back to it is that life is to be *lived*. He hates to see young people going into 'retirement' early in life; that is, young people who settle for a lacklustre, comfortable existence instead of taking up life's invitation to let their own lives be transformed by the Gospel of Jesus and, then, in turn, transforming the world around them, making of it a world inspired by high ideals.

Pope Francis encourages young people to be open, to let themselves be surprised by what God might want to do in their lives. He shares his own particular story, but each person will have his or her own story. When he was seventeen-years-old, it happened one day that, as he was about to go out with friends, he decided to go into a church first. He met a priest there who inspired great confidence, and so he felt the desire to open his heart in Confession. That meeting changed his life! He discovered that when we open our hearts with humility and transparency, we can contemplate God's mercy in a very concrete way. He felt certain that, in the person of that priest, God was already waiting for him even before he took the step of entering that church. We keep looking for God, but God is there before us, always looking for us, and he finds us first. For the young Argentinian, Jorge Bergoglio, the future Pope, it was an experience that he never forgot: God is waiting for you! God is a Father and he is always waiting for us!

When, in January 2016, the Irish Bishops met Pope Francis in the Vatican for a conversation that lasted for around two hours, the Pope spoke several times of young people. It was clear he cares so much for them. He recognises the challenges they face. In Ireland young people often feel iffy about the Church because of the scandals of recent years. And yet Pope Francis has great confidence in young people. His great love for them and his understanding of young people struck the Bishops very much.

On returning from World Youth Day in Poland and again after the Irish Bishops meeting with the Pope, I felt it would be good to put together a book that would give young people an opportunity to listen directly to conversations between young people and Pope Francis. I am grateful to Veritas for publishing this short book. Many of the texts contained here come from the World Youth Day 2016 in Kraków. But I have also included some question and answer sessions that Pope Francis has had with young people in various parts of the world during his apostolic visits.

Here and there I have inserted a few subheadings to facilitate easier reading of the text. As you'll notice most of the texts are transcriptions of Pope Francis' own words spoken on the various occasions mentioned rather than the official speeches that he might have prepared for those occasions beforehand. I've edited hardly anything so that we can 'hear' Pope Francis speak spontaneously.

Pope Francis certainly raises the bar high! Those who were part of the million-plus crowd at Kraków will recall vividly Francis saying:

The times we live in do not call for young 'couch potatoes', but for young people with shoes, or better, boots laced. The times we live in require only active players on the field, and there is no room for those who sit on the bench. Today's world demands that you be a protagonist of history because life is always beautiful when we choose to live it fully, when we choose to leave a mark.

I hope that in reading this book, young people will find themselves in conversation with Pope Francis. He certainly wants to reach each young man and woman, personally and uniquely. As a remarkable instrument of the Holy Spirit in our time, he has something important to say to each of us.

† Brendan Leahy

CHAPTER ONE

Two Things I've Learned in Life

Following his opening comments at the welcoming ceremony of World Youth Day 2016 in Kraków, Pope Francis continued by sharing two things he had learned in life with regard to young people.[1]

In my years as a bishop, I have learned many things, but I want to share one with you now: nothing is more beautiful than seeing the enthusiasm, dedication, zeal and energy with which so many young people live their lives. This is beautiful! And where does this beauty come from? When Jesus touches a young person's heart, he or she becomes capable of truly great things. It is exciting to listen to you share your dreams, your questions and your impatience with those who say that things cannot change, those whom I call 'quietists' (who say) 'nothing can change' …

Today the Church looks to you, and I would add, the world looks to you, and wants to learn from you, to be reassured that the Father's Mercy has an ever-youthful face and constantly invites us to be part of his kingdom.

Knowing your enthusiasm for mission, I repeat: mercy always has a youthful face! Because a merciful heart is motivated to move beyond its comfort zone. A merciful heart can go out and meet others; it is ready to embrace everyone. A merciful heart is able to be a place of refuge for those who are without a home or have lost their home; it is able to build a home and a family for those forced to emigrate; it knows the meaning of tenderness and compassion. A merciful heart can share its bread with the hungry and welcome refugees and migrants.

To say the word 'mercy' along with you is to speak of opportunity, future, commitment, trust, openness, hospitality, compassion and dreams. But are you able to dream? [The Young People reply: Yes!] When the heart is open and able to dream, there is room for mercy...

Don't Go into Early Retirement!

Let me tell you another thing I have learned over these years. I do not want to offend anyone, but it pains me to meet young people who seem to have opted for 'early retirement'. This pains me. Young people who seem to retire at twenty-three, twenty-four, twenty-five years of age. This pains me. I worry when I see young people who have 'thrown in the towel' before the game has even begun, who are defeated even before they begin to play. I am saddened to see young people who walk around glumly as if life had no meaning. Deep down, young people like this are bored ... and boring, who bore others, and this upsets me.

But it is also hard, and troubling, to see young people who waste their lives looking for thrills or a feeling of being alive by taking dark paths and in the end having to pay for it ... and pay dearly. Think of so many young people you know who have chosen this path. It is disturbing to see young people squandering some of the best years of their lives, wasting their energies running after peddlers of false illusions, and they do exist (where I come from, we call them 'vendors of smoke'), who rob you of what is best in you. This pains me. I am sure that among you there are no such persons, but I want to tell you: there are young people that have gone into retirement, who have thrown in the towel before the game has even begun, there are young people who are enthralled by false illusions and end up in nothingness …

To find fulfilment, to gain new life, there is a way, a way that is not for sale, that cannot be purchased, a way that is not a thing or an object, but a person. His name is Jesus Christ. I ask you: can you buy Jesus Christ? Can Jesus Christ be bought at the shops? Jesus Christ is a gift, a gift from the Father, the gift from our Father …

Jesus can give you true passion for life. Jesus can inspire us not to settle for less, but to give the very best of ourselves. Jesus challenges us, spurs us on and helps us keep trying whenever we are tempted to give up. Jesus pushes us to keep our sights high and to dream of great things.

I try but So Many Times I fall Down

You might say to me, 'but Father, it is so difficult to dream of great things, it is so difficult to rise up, to be always moving forwards and upwards. Father, I am weak, I fall, and I try but so many times I fall down'. Mountaineers, as they climb mountains, sing a very beautiful song whose words go like this: 'in the art of climbing, it is not important that you do not fall down, but that you do not stay down'. If you are weak, if you fall, look up a little for there is Jesus' hand extended to you as he says: 'Rise up, come with me'. 'And what if I fall again?' Rise again. 'And what if I fall yet again?' Rise yet again. Peter once asked the Lord: 'Lord, how many times?' And the reply came: 'seventy times seven'. The hand of Jesus is always extended, ready to lift us up again when we fall …

Jesus Wants to Stop and Enter our Home

In the Gospel, we heard how Jesus, on his way to Jerusalem, stopped at a home – the home of Martha, Mary and Lazarus – and was welcomed. He stopped, went in and spent time with them. The two women welcomed him because they knew he was open and attentive. Our many jobs and responsibilities can make us a bit like Martha: busy, scattered, constantly running from place to place … but we can also be like Mary: whenever we see a beautiful landscape, or look at a video from a friend on our mobile phone, we can stop and think, stop and listen … In these days, Jesus wants to stop and enter our home: your home, my home, enter into our hearts; Jesus will look at us hurrying about with all our concerns, as he did with Martha … and he will wait for us to listen to him, like Mary, to make space for him amid the bustle …

Whoever welcomes Jesus learns to love as Jesus does. So he asks us if we want a full life. And in his name, I ask you: do you want a full life? Start right this moment by letting yourself be open and attentive! Because happiness is sown and blossoms in mercy. That is his answer, his offer, his challenge, his adventure: mercy. Mercy always has a youthful face. Like that of Mary of Bethany, who sat as a disciple at the feet of

Jesus and joyfully listened to his words, since she knew that there she would find peace. Like that of Mary of Nazareth, whose daring 'Yes' launched her on the adventure of mercy. All generations would call her blessed; to all of us she is the 'Mother of Mercy'…

A Prayer to Help Us

All together, let us ask the Lord, each repeating in the silence of his or her heart: 'Lord, launch us on the adventure of mercy! Launch us on the adventure of building bridges and tearing down walls, be they barriers or barbed wire. Launch us on the adventure of helping the poor, those who feel lonely and abandoned, or no longer find meaning in their lives. Launch us on the journey of accompanying those who do not know you, and telling them carefully and respectfully your Name, the reason for our faith. Send us, like Mary of Bethany, to listen attentively to those we do not understand, those of other cultures and peoples, even those we are afraid of because we consider them a threat. Make us attentive to our elders, to our grandparents, as Mary of Nazareth was to Elizabeth, in order to learn from their wisdom … Here we are, Lord! Send us to share your merciful loves …'

CHAPTER TWO

Where is God?

During the Way of the Cross ceremony at World Youth Day 2016 in Kraków, Pope Francis took up words we find in Matthew's Gospel: 'I was hungry and you gave me food, I was thirsty and you gave me something to drink, I was a stranger and you welcomed me, I was naked and you gave me clothing, I was sick and you took care of me, I was in prison and you visited me' (Mt 25:35-36). He addressed the questions we have when faced with the many aspects of suffering in today's world.[2]

Questions that Humanly Speaking have no Answer

These words of Jesus answer the question that arises so often in our minds and hearts: 'Where is God?' Where is God, if evil is present in our world, if there are men and women who are hungry and thirsty, homeless, exiles and refugees? Where is God, when innocent persons die as a result of violence, terrorism and war? Where is God, when cruel diseases break the bonds of life and affection? Or when children are exploited and demeaned, and they too suffer from grave illness? Where is God, amid the anguish of those who doubt and are troubled in spirit? These are questions that humanly speaking have no answer. We can only look to Jesus and ask him. And Jesus' answer is this: 'God is in them'. Jesus is in them; he suffers in them and deeply identifies with each of them. He is so closely united to them as to form with them, as it were, 'one body'.

Jesus himself chose to identify with these our brothers and sisters enduring pain and anguish by agreeing to tread the 'way of sorrows' that led to Calvary. By dying on the cross, he surrendered himself into the hands of the Father, taking upon himself and in himself, with self-sacrificing love, the physical, moral and spiritual wounds of all humanity. By embracing the wood of the cross, Jesus embraced the nakedness, the hunger and thirst, the loneliness, pain and death of men and women of all times …

Following Jesus with Works of Mercy

By following Jesus along the Way of the Cross, we have once again realised the importance of imitating him through the fourteen *works of mercy*. These help us to be open to God's mercy, to implore the grace to appreciate that without mercy we can do nothing; without mercy, neither I nor you nor any of us can do a thing. Let us first consider the seven **corporal** works of mercy: feeding the hungry, giving drink to the thirsty, clothing the naked, sheltering the homeless, visiting the sick and those in prison, and burying the dead. Freely we have received, so freely let us give. We are called to serve the crucified Jesus in all those who are marginalised, to touch his sacred flesh in those who are disadvantaged, in those who hunger and thirst, in the naked and imprisoned, the sick and unemployed, in those who are persecuted, refugees and migrants. There we find our God; there we touch the Lord. Jesus himself told us this when he explained the criterion on which we will be judged: whenever we do these things to the least of our brothers and sisters, we do them to him (cf. Mt 25:31-46).

After the corporal works of mercy come the **spiritual** works: counselling the doubtful, instructing the ignorant, admonishing sinners, consoling the afflicted, pardoning offences, bearing wrongs patiently, praying for the living and the dead. In welcoming the outcast who suffer physically and in welcoming sinners who suffer spiritually, our credibility as Christians is at stake. Not in ideas, but in our actions.

Be Sowers of Hope

Humanity today needs men and women, and especially young people like yourselves, who do not wish to live their lives 'halfway', young people ready to spend their lives freely in service to those of their brothers and sisters who are poorest and most vulnerable, in imitation of Christ who gave himself completely for our salvation. In the face of evil, suffering and sin, the only response possible for a disciple of Jesus is the gift of self, even of one's own life, in imitation of Christ; it is the attitude of service. Unless those who call themselves Christians live to serve, their lives serve no good purpose. By their lives, they deny Jesus Christ.

The Lord once more asks you to be in the forefront in serving others. He wants to make of you *a concrete response* to the needs and sufferings of humanity. He wants you to be signs of his merciful love for our time! To enable you to carry out this mission, he shows you the way of personal commitment and self-sacrifice. It is the Way of the Cross. The Way of the Cross is the way of fidelity in following Jesus to the end, in the often dramatic situations of everyday life. It is a way that fears no lack of success, ostracism or solitude, because it fills ours hearts with the fullness of Jesus. The Way of the Cross is the way of God's own life, his 'style', which Jesus brings even to the pathways of a society at times divided, unjust and corrupt.

The Way of the Cross is not an exercise in sadomasochism; the Way of the Cross alone defeats sin, evil and death, for it leads to the radiant light of Christ's Resurrection and opens the horizons of a new and fuller life. It is the way of hope, the way of the future. Those who take up this way with generosity and faith give hope to the future and to humanity. Those who take up this way with generosity and faith sow seeds of hope. I want you to be sowers of hope.

Dear young people, on that Good Friday many disciples went back crestfallen to their homes. Others chose to go out to the country to forget the cross. I ask you: but I want each of you to answer in silence in the depths of your heart. How do you want to go back this evening to your own homes, to the places where you are staying, to your tents? How do you want to go back this evening to be alone with your thoughts? The world is watching us. Each of you has to answer the challenge that this question sets before you.

CHAPTER THREE

Don't be Couch Potatoes!

On 30 July, during World Youth Day 2016, more than a million young people walked about fifteen kilometres from the centre of Kraków to the 'Campus Misericordia' (the 'Field of Mercy'), the site for vigil and Mass with Pope Francis. It was an amazing sight to see so many people waving their flags, singing, cheering and helping one another so enthusiastically. The Pope too enjoyed the occasion. But he also had a strong message to impart. During his talk at the prayer vigil he encouraged young people resist being dominated by others who would like to control them. That means not living life as 'couch potatoes' and striving for the freedom that enables young people to make a mark in this world.

The vigil began with three powerful testimonies. Natalia, a young Polish woman from Lodz, spoke of her experience of encountering the love of God through the Sacrament of Reconciliation after twenty years 'of not having anything in common with the Church'. Miguel, a young Paraguayan and former drug addict, discovered God's calling by helping others at a halfway house. Rand Mittri from Aleppo, Syria told of the violence and war that has caused so many of its people to become either internally displaced persons or refugees seeking asylum in neighbouring countries such as Iraq, Jordan, Lebanon.[3]

Our Unity in Prayer

Dear Young Friends, good evening! It is good to be here with you at this prayer vigil! At the end of her powerful and moving witness, Rand asked something of us. She said: 'I earnestly ask you to pray for my beloved country'. Her story, involving war, grief and loss, ended with a request for prayers. Is there a better way for us to begin our vigil than by praying?

We have come here from different parts of the world, from different continents, countries, languages, cultures and peoples. Some of us are sons and daughters of nations that may be at odds and engaged in various conflicts or even open war. Others of us come from countries that may be at 'peace', free of war and conflict, where most of the terrible things occurring in our world are simply a story on the evening news.

But think about it. For us, here, today, coming from different parts of the world, the suffering and the wars that many young people experience are no longer anonymous, something we read about in the papers. They have a name, they have a face, they have a story, they are close at hand. Today the war in Syria has caused pain and suffering for so many people, for so many young people like our brave friend Rand, who has come here and asked us to pray for her beloved country.

Some situations seem distant until in some way we touch them. We don't appreciate certain things because we only see them on the screen of a cell phone or a computer. But when we come into contact with life, with people's lives, not just images on a screen, something powerful happens. We all feel the need to get involved. To see that there are no more 'forgotten cities', to use Rand's words, or brothers and sisters of ours 'surrounded by death and killing', completely helpless.

Dear friends, I ask that we join in prayer for the sufferings of all the victims of war, of this war today in the world. Once and for all, may we realise that nothing justifies shedding the blood of a brother or sister; that nothing is more precious than the person next to us. In asking you to pray for this, I would also like to thank Natalia and Miguel for sharing their own battles and inner conflicts. You told us about your struggles, and about how you succeeded in overcoming them. Both of you are a living sign of what God's mercy wants to accomplish in us.

This is no time for denouncing anyone or fighting. We do not want to tear down, we do not want to give insult. We have no desire to conquer hatred with more hatred, violence with more violence, terror with more terror. We are here today because the Lord has called us together. Our response to a world at war has a name: its name is fraternity, its name is brotherhood, its name is communion, its name is family.

We celebrate the fact that coming from different cultures, we have come together to pray. Let our best word, our best argument, be our unity in prayer. Let us take a moment of silence and pray ...

Fear and the Feeling of Being Paralysed

As we were praying, I thought of the Apostles on the day of Pentecost. Picturing them can help us come to appreciate all that God dreams of accomplishing in our lives, in us and with us. That day, the disciples were together behind locked doors, out of fear. They felt threatened, surrounded by an atmosphere of persecution that had cornered them in a little room and left them silent and paralysed. Fear had taken hold of them. Then, in that situation, something spectacular, something grandiose, occurred. The Holy Spirit and tongues as of fire came to rest upon each of them, propelling them towards an undreamt-of adventure. This brings about a total change!

We have heard three testimonies. Our hearts were touched by their stories, their lives. We have seen how, like the disciples, they experienced similar moments, living through times of great fear, when it seemed like everything was falling apart. The fear and anguish born of knowing that leaving home might mean never again seeing their loved ones, the fear of not feeling appreciated or loved, the fear of having no choices. They shared with us the same experience the disciples had; they felt the kind of fear that only leads to one thing.

Where does fear lead us? The feeling of being closed in on oneself, trapped. Once we feel that way, our fear starts to fester and is inevitably joined by its 'twin sister', paralysis: the feeling of being paralysed. Thinking that in this world, in our cities and our communities, there is no longer any room to grow, to dream, to create, to gaze at new horizons – in a word to live – is one of the worst things that can happen to us in life, and especially at a younger age. When we are paralysed, we miss the magic of encountering others, making friends, sharing dreams, walking at the side of others. This paralysis distances us from others, it prevents us from taking each other's hand …

Confusing Happiness with a Sofa!

But in life there is another, even more dangerous, kind of paralysis. It is not easy to put our finger on it. I like to describe it as the paralysis that comes from confusing happiness with a sofa. In other words, to think that in order to be happy all we need is a good sofa. A sofa that makes us feel comfortable, calm, safe. A sofa like one of those we have nowadays with a built-in massage unit to put us to sleep. A sofa that promises us hours of comfort so we can escape to the world of videogames and spend all kinds of time in front of a computer screen. A sofa that keeps us safe from any kind of pain and fear. A sofa that allows us to stay home without needing to work at, or worry about, anything. 'Sofa-happiness'! That is probably the most harmful and insidious form of paralysis, which can cause the greatest harm to young people.

And why does this happen? Because, little by little, without even realising it, we start to nod off, to grow drowsy and dull. The other day, I spoke about young people who go into retirement at the age of twenty; today I speak about young persons who nod off, grow drowsy and dull, while others – perhaps more alert than we are, but not necessarily better – decide our future for us. For many people in fact, it is much easier and better to have drowsy and dull kids who confuse happiness with a sofa. For many people, that is more convenient than having young people who are alert and searching, trying to respond to God's dream and to all the restlessness present in the human heart. I ask you: do you want to be young people who nod off, who are drowsy and dull? Do you want others to decide your future for you? Do you want to be free? Do you want to be alert? Do you want to work hard for your future?

Leave a Mark; Defend our Freedom

The truth, though, is something else. Dear young people, we didn't come into this world to 'vegetate', to take it easy, to make our lives a comfortable sofa to fall asleep on. No, we came for another reason: to leave a mark. It is very sad to pass through life without leaving a mark. But when we opt for ease and convenience, for confusing happiness with consumption, then we end up paying a high price indeed: we lose our freedom. We are not free to leave a mark. We lose our freedom. This is the high price we pay. There are so many people who do not want the young to be free; there are so many people who do not wish you well, who want you to be drowsy and dull, and never free! No, this must not be so! We must defend our freedom!

This is itself a great form of paralysis, whenever we start thinking that happiness is the same as comfort and convenience, that being happy means going through life asleep or on tranquillizers, that the only way to be happy is to live in a haze. Certainly, drugs are bad, but there are plenty of other socially acceptable drugs, that can end up enslaving us just the same. One way or the other, they rob us of our greatest treasure: our freedom. They strip us of our freedom.

Trade in the Sofa for a Pair of Walking Shoes

My friends, Jesus is the Lord of risk, he is the Lord of the eternal 'more'. Jesus is not the Lord of comfort, security and ease. Following Jesus demands a good dose of courage, a readiness to trade in the sofa for a pair of walking shoes and to set out on new and uncharted paths. To blaze trails that open up new horizons capable of spreading joy, the joy that is born of God's love and wells up in your hearts with every act of mercy.

To take the path of the 'craziness' of our God, who teaches us to encounter him in the hungry, the thirsty, the naked, the sick, the friend in trouble, the prisoner, the refugee and the migrant, and our neighbours who feel abandoned. To take the path of our God, who encourages us to be politicians, thinkers, social activists. The God who encourages us to devise an economy marked by greater solidarity than our own. In all the settings in which you find yourselves, God's love invites you to bring the Good News, making of your own lives a gift to him and to others. This means being courageous, this means being free!

The World Can be Different; God Expects Something of You

You might say to me: Father, that is not for everybody, but just for a chosen few. True, and those chosen are all who are ready to share their lives with others. Just as the Holy Spirit transformed the hearts of the disciples on the day of Pentecost, and they were paralysed, so he did with our friends who shared their testimonies. I will use your own words, Miguel. You told us that in the 'Facenda' [centre for those in drug recovery] on the day they entrusted you with the responsibility for helping make the house run better, you began to understand that God was asking something of you. That is when things began to change.

That is the secret, dear friends, and all of us are called to share in it. God expects something from you. Have you understood this? God expects something from you, God wants something from you. God hopes in you. God comes to break down all our fences. He comes to open the doors of our lives, our dreams, our ways of seeing things. God comes to break open everything that keeps you closed in. He is encouraging you to dream. He wants to make you see that, with you, the world can be different. For the fact is, unless you offer the best of yourselves, the world will never be different. This is the challenge.

The times we live in do not call for young 'couch potatoes', but for young people with shoes, or better, boots laced. The times we live in require only active players on the field, and there is no room for those who sit on the bench. Today's world demands that you be a protagonist of history because life is always beautiful when we choose to live it fully, when we choose to leave a mark. History today calls us to defend our dignity and not to let others decide our future. No! We must decide our future, you must decide your future!

As he did on Pentecost, the Lord wants to work one of the greatest miracles we can experience; he wants to turn your hands, my hands, our hands, into signs of reconciliation, of communion, of creation. He wants your hands to continue building the world of today. And he wants to build that world with you. And what is your response? Yes or no?

You might say to me: Father, but I have my limits, I am a sinner, what can I do? When the Lord calls us, he doesn't worry about what we are, what we have been, or what we have done or not done. Quite the opposite. When he calls us, he is thinking about everything we have to give, all the love we are capable of spreading. His bets are on the future, on tomorrow. Jesus is pointing you to the future, and never to the museum.

So today, my friends, Jesus is inviting you, calling you, to leave your mark on life, to leave a mark on history, your own and that of many others as well.

Have the Courage to Teach Us!

Life nowadays tells us that it is much easier to concentrate on what divides us, what keeps us apart. People try to make us believe that being closed in on ourselves is the best way to keep safe from harm. Today, we adults need you to teach us, as you are doing today, how to live in diversity, in dialogue, to experience multiculturalism not as a threat but an opportunity. You are an opportunity for the future. Have the courage to teach us, have the courage to show us that it is easier to build bridges than walls!

We need to learn this. Together we ask that you challenge us to take the path of fraternity. May you point the finger at us, if we choose the path of walls, the path of enmity, the path of war. To build bridges ... Do you know the first bridge that has to be built? It is a bridge that we can build here and now – by reaching out and taking each other's hand. Come on, build it now. Build this human bridge, take each other's hand, all of you: it is the first of bridges, it is the human bridge, it is the first, it is the model. There is always a risk, as I said the other day, of offering your hand and no one taking it. But in life we need to take a risk, for the person who does not take a risk never wins. With this bridge we can move forwards. Here, this is the primordial bridge: take each other's hand. Thank you. This is a great bridge of brotherhood, and would that the powers of this world might learn to build it ... not for pictures and ulterior motives, but for building ever bigger bridges. May this human bridge be the beginning of many, many others; in that way, it will leave a mark.

Today Jesus, who is the way, the truth and the life, is calling you, you, and you to leave your mark on history. He, who is life, is asking each of you to leave a mark that brings life to your own history and that of many others. He, who is truth, is asking you to abandon the paths of rejection, division and emptiness. Are you up to this? ... What answer will you give, and I'd like to see it, with your hands and with your feet, to the Lord, who is the way, the truth and the life? Are you up to this? May the Lord bless your dreams. Thank you!

CHAPTER FOUR

Obstacles We all Face

The final Mass at World Youth Day 2016 in Kraków was held on a Sunday morning of glorious sunshine. More than 1.6 million people attended; many of them had slept under the stars following the previous night's prayer vigil. Based on the Gospel read at the Mass, Pope Francis reflected on Zacchaeus' encounter with Jesus. He outlined three obstacles we may face in our own lives when it comes to meeting Jesus.

An Amazing Encounter

Dear young people, you have come to Kraków to meet Jesus. Today's Gospel speaks to us of just such a meeting between Jesus and a man named Zacchaeus, in Jericho (cf. Lk 19:1-10). There Jesus does not simply preach or greet people; as the Evangelist tells us, he *passed through* the city (v. 1). In other words, Jesus wants to draw near to us personally, to accompany our journey to its end, so that his life and our life can truly meet.

An amazing encounter then takes place, with Zacchaeus, the chief 'publican' or tax collector. Zacchaeus was thus a wealthy collaborator of the hated Roman occupiers, someone who exploited his own people, someone who, because of his ill repute, could not even approach the Master. His encounter with Jesus changed his life, just as it has changed, and can daily still change, each of our lives. But Zacchaeus had to face a number of obstacles in order to meet Jesus. It was not easy for him; he had to face *a number of obstacles. At least three of these* can also say something to us.

Not Accepting Ourselves as We Are

The *first* obstacle is smallness of stature. Zacchaeus couldn't see the Master because he was small. Even today we can risk not getting close to Jesus because we don't feel big enough, because we don't think ourselves worthy. This is a great temptation; it has to do not only with self-esteem, but with faith itself. For faith tells us that we are 'children of God … that is what we are' (1 Jn 3:1). We have been created in God's own image; Jesus has taken upon himself our humanity and his heart will never be separated from us; the Holy Spirit wants to dwell within us. We have been called to be happy for ever with God!

That is our real 'stature', our spiritual identity: we are God's beloved children, always. So you can see that not to accept ourselves, to live glumly, to be negative, means not to recognise our deepest identity. It is like walking away when God wants to look at me, trying to spoil his dream for me. God loves us the way we are, and no sin, fault or mistake of ours makes him change his mind.

As far as Jesus is concerned – as the Gospel shows – no one is unworthy of, or far from, his thoughts. No one is insignificant. He loves all of us with a special love; for him all of us are important: *you* are important! God counts on you for what you are, not for what you possess. In his eyes the clothes you wear or the kind of cell phone you use are of absolutely no concern. He doesn't care whether you are stylish or not; he cares about you, just as you are! In his eyes, you are precious, and your value is inestimable.

At times in our lives, we aim lower rather than higher. At those times, it is good to realise that God remains faithful, even obstinate, in his love for us. The fact is, he loves us even more than we love ourselves. He believes in us even more than we believe in ourselves. He is always 'cheering us on'; he is our biggest fan. He is there for us, waiting with patience and hope, even when we turn in on ourselves and brood over our troubles and past injuries. But such brooding is unworthy of our spiritual stature! It is a kind of *virus* infecting and blocking everything; it closes doors and prevents us from getting up and starting over. God, on the other hand, is hopelessly hopeful!

He believes that we can always get up, and he hates to see us glum and gloomy. It is sad to see young people who are glum. Because we are always his beloved sons and daughters let us be mindful of this at the dawn of each new day. It will do us good to pray every morning: 'Lord, I thank you for loving me; I am sure that you love me; help me to be in love with my own life!' Not with my faults, that need to be corrected, but with life itself, which is a great gift, for it is a time to love and to be loved.

The Paralysis of Shame

Zacchaeus faced a *second* obstacle in meeting Jesus: the paralysis of shame. We can imagine what was going on in his heart before he climbed that sycamore. It must have been quite a struggle – on one hand, a healthy curiosity and desire to know Jesus; on the other, the risk of appearing completely ridiculous. Zacchaeus was a public figure, a man of power, but deeply hated. He knew that, in trying to climb that tree, he would have become a laughingstock to all. Yet he mastered his shame, because the attraction of Jesus was more powerful.

You know what happens when someone is so attractive that we fall in love with them: we end up ready to do things we would never have even thought of doing. Something similar took place in the heart of Zacchaeus, when he realised that Jesus was so important that he would do anything for him, since Jesus alone could pull him out of the mire of sin and discontent. The paralysis of shame did not have the upper hand.

The Gospel tells us that Zacchaeus 'ran ahead', 'climbed' the tree, and then, when Jesus called him, he 'hurried down' (vv. 4, 6). He took a risk, he put his life on the line. For us too, this is the secret of joy: not to stifle a healthy curiosity, but to take a risk, because life is not meant to be tucked away. When it comes to Jesus, we cannot sit around waiting with arms folded; he offers us life – we can't respond by thinking about it or 'texting' a few words!

Dear young friends, don't be ashamed to bring everything to the Lord in confession, especially your weaknesses, your struggles and your sins. He will surprise you with his forgiveness and his peace. Don't be afraid to say 'yes' to him with all your heart, to respond generously and to follow him!

Don't let your soul grow numb, but aim for the goal of a beautiful love which also demands sacrifice. Say a firm 'no' to the narcotic of success at any cost and the sedative of worrying only about yourself and your own comfort.

Fear of the Crowd

After his small stature, after the paralysis of shame, there was a *third* obstacle that Zacchaeus had to face. It was no longer an interior one, but was all around him. It was the *grumbling of the crowd*, who first blocked him and then criticised him: How could Jesus have entered his house, the house of a sinner! How truly hard it is to welcome Jesus, how hard it is to accept a 'God who is rich in mercy' (Eph 2:4)!

People will try to block you, to make you think that God is distant, rigid and insensitive, good to the good and bad to the bad. Instead, our heavenly Father 'makes his sun rise on the evil and on the good' (Mt 5:45). He demands of us real courage: the courage to be more powerful than evil by loving everyone, even our enemies. People may laugh at you because you believe in the gentle and unassuming power of mercy. But do not be afraid. Think of the motto of these days: 'Blessed are the merciful, for they will receive mercy' (Mt 5:7).

People may judge you to be dreamers, because you believe in a new humanity, one that rejects hatred between peoples, one that refuses to see borders as barriers and can cherish its own traditions without being self-centred or small-minded. Don't be discouraged: with a smile and open arms, you proclaim hope and you are a blessing for our one human family, which here you represent so beautifully!

That day the crowd judged Zacchaeus; they looked him over, up and down. But Jesus did otherwise: he gazed up at him (v. 5). Jesus looks beyond the faults and sees the person. He does not halt before bygone evil, but sees future good. His gaze remains constant, even when it is not met; it seeks the way of unity and communion. In no case does it halt at appearances, but looks to the heart.

Jesus looks to our hearts, your heart, my heart. With this gaze of Jesus, you can help bring about another humanity, without looking for acknowledgement but seeking goodness for its own sake, content to maintain a pure heart and to fight peaceably for honesty and justice. Don't stop at the surface of things; distrust the worldly cult of appearances, cosmetic attempts to improve our looks. Instead, 'download' the best 'link' of all, that of a heart which sees and transmits goodness without growing weary. The joy that you have freely received from God, please, freely give away (cf. Mt 10:8): so many people are waiting for it! So many are waiting for it from you.

God's Memory is not a 'Hard Disk'!

Finally let us listen to the words that Jesus spoke to Zacchaeus, which seem meant for us today, for each one of us: 'Come down, for I must stay at your house today' (v. 5). 'Come down, for I must stay with you today. Open to me the door of your heart'. Jesus extends the same invitation to you: 'I must stay at your house today'. We can say that World Youth Day *begins today and continues tomorrow, in your homes*, since that is where Jesus wants to meet you from now on. The Lord doesn't want to remain in this beautiful city, or in cherished memories alone. He wants to enter your homes, to dwell in your daily lives: in your studies, your first years of work, your friendships and affections, your hopes and dreams. How greatly he desires that you bring all this to him in prayer! How much he hopes that, in all the 'contacts' and 'chats' of each day, pride of place be given to the golden thread of prayer! How much he wants his word to be able to speak to you day after day, so that you can make his Gospel your own, so that it can serve as a compass for you on the highways of life!

In asking to come to your house, Jesus *calls you*, as he did Zacchaeus, *by name*. All of us, Jesus calls by name. Your name is precious to him. The name 'Zacchaeus' would have made people back then, in the language of the time, think of God. Trust the memory of God: his memory is not a 'hard disk' that 'saves' and 'archives' all our data, his memory is a heart filled with tender compassion, one that finds joy in 'erasing' in us every trace of evil. May we too now try to imitate the faithful memory of God and treasure the good things we have received in these days. In silence, let us remember this encounter, let us preserve the memory of the presence of God and his word, and let us listen once more to the voice of Jesus as he calls us by name. So let us now pray silently, remembering and thanking the Lord who wanted us to be here and has come here to meet us.

CHAPTER FIVE

It's Important to Dream

At a gathering of young people in Havana, Cuba, Pope Francis listened carefully to what young people were saying to him, taking notes and then responding to their comments.[4]

Dream

You are standing up and I am sitting. How rude! But you know why I am sitting; it is because I was taking notes on some of the things which our companion here was saying. Those are the things I want to talk about. One really striking word he used was 'dream'. A Latin American writer once said that we all have two eyes: one of flesh and another of glass. With the eye of flesh, we see what is in front of us. With the eye of glass, we see what we dream of. Beautiful, isn't it?

In the daily reality of life, there has to be room for dreaming. A young person incapable of dreaming is cut off, self-enclosed. Everyone sometimes dreams of things which are never going to happen. But dream them anyway, desire them, seek new horizons, be open to great things.

I'm not sure if you use this word in Cuba, but in Argentina we say: 'Don't be a pushover!' Don't bend or yield; open up.

Open up and dream! Dream that with you the world can be different. Dream that if you give your best, you are going to help make this world a different place. Don't forget to dream! If you get carried away and dream too much, life will cut you short. It makes no difference; dream anyway, and share your dreams. Talk about the great things you wish for, because the greater your ability to dream, the farther you will have gone; even if life cuts you short half way, you will still have gone a great distance. So, first of all, dream!

If You Are Different Than I Am, Then Why Don't We Talk?

You said something which I had wrote down and underlined. You said that we have to know how to welcome and accept those who think differently than we do. Honestly, sometimes we are very closed. We shut ourselves up in our little world: 'Either things go my way or not at all'. And you went even further. You said that we must not become enclosed in our little ideological or religious 'worlds'... that we need to outgrow forms of individualism.

When a religion becomes a 'little world', it loses the best that it has, it stops worshiping God, believing in God. It becomes a little world of words, of prayers, of 'I am good and you are bad', of moral rules and regulations. When I have my ideology, my way of thinking, and you have yours, I lock myself up in this little world of ideology.

Open hearts and open minds. If you are different than I am, then why don't we talk? Why do we always throw stones at one another over what separates us, what makes us different? Why don't we extend a hand where we have common ground? Why not try to speak about what we have in common, and then we can talk about where we differ. But I'm saying 'talk'; I'm not saying 'fight'. I am not saying retreat into our 'little worlds', to use your word. But this can only happen when I am able to speak about what I have in common with the other person, about things we can work on together.

Social Friendship

In Buenos Aires, in a new parish in an extremely poor area, a group of university students were building some rooms for the parish. So the parish priest said to me: 'Why don't you come one Saturday and I'll introduce them to you'. They were building on Saturdays and Sundays. They were young men and women from the university. So I arrived, I saw them and they were introduced to me: 'This is the architect. He's Jewish. This one is Communist. This one is a practising Catholic'. They were all different, yet they were all working for the common good.

This is called social friendship, where everyone works for the common good. Social enmity instead destroys. A family is destroyed by enmity. A country is destroyed by enmity. The world is destroyed by enmity. And the greatest enmity is war. Today we see that the world is being destroyed by war, because people are incapable of sitting down and talking. 'Good, let's negotiate. What can we do together? Where are we going to draw the line? But let's not kill any more people'. Where there is division, there is death: the death of the soul, since we are killing our ability to come together. We are killing social friendship. And this is what I'm asking you today: to find ways of building social friendship'.

What is Hope?

Then there was another word you said: 'hope'. The young are the hope of every people; we hear this all the time. But what is hope? Does it mean being optimistic? No. Optimism is a state of mind. Tomorrow, you wake up in a bad mood and you're not optimistic at all; you see everything in a bad light. Hope is something more. Hope involves suffering. Hope can accept suffering as part of building something; it is able to sacrifice.

Are you able to sacrifice for the future, or do you simply want to live for the day and let those yet to come fend for themselves? Hope is fruitful. Hope gives life. Are you able to be life-giving? Or are you going to be young people who are spiritually barren, incapable of giving life to others, incapable of building social friendship, incapable of building a nation, incapable of doing great things?

Hope is fruitful. Hope comes from working, from having a job. Here I would mention a very grave problem in Europe: the number of young people who are unemployed. There are countries in Europe where 40 per cent of young people twenty-five years and younger are unemployed. I am thinking of one country. In another country, it is 47 per cent and in another still, 50 per cent.

Clearly, when a people is not concerned with providing work to its young – and when I say 'a people', I don't mean governments; I mean the entire people who ought to be concerned whether these young people have jobs or not – that people has no future. Young people become part of the throwaway culture and all of us know that today, under the rule of mammon, things get thrown away and people get thrown away.

Children are thrown away because they are not wanted, or killed before they are born. The elderly are thrown away – I'm speaking about the world in general – because they are no longer productive. In some countries, euthanasia is legal, but in so many others there is a hidden, covert euthanasia. Young people are thrown away because they are not given work. So then, what is left for a young person who has no work? When a country – a people – does not create employment opportunities for its young, what is left for these young people if not forms of addiction, or suicide, or going off in search of armies of destruction in order to make war.

This throwaway culture is harming us all; it is taking away our hope. And this is what you asked for in the name of young people: 'We want hope'. A hope which requires effort, hard work, and which bears fruit; a hope which gives us work and saves us from the throwaway culture. A hope which unites people, all people, because a people can join in looking to the future and in building social friendship – for all their differences – such a people has hope.

For me, meeting a young person without hope is, as I once said, like meeting a young retiree. There are young people who seem to have retired at the age of twenty-two. They are young people filled with existential dreariness, young people who have surrendered to defeatism, young people who whine and run away from life. The path of hope is not an easy one. And it can't be taken alone. There is an African proverb which says: 'If you want to go quickly, walk alone, but if you want to go far, walk with another'.

A Culture of Encounter

So this is what I have to say to you, the young people of Cuba. For all your different ways of thinking and seeing things, I would like you to walk with others, together, looking for hope, seeking the future and the nobility of your homeland.

We began with the word 'dream', and I would like to conclude with another word that you said and which I myself often use: 'the culture of encounter'. Please, let us not 'dis-encounter' one another. Let us go side by side with one other, as one. Encountering one another, even though we may think differently, even though we may feel differently. There is something bigger than us, it is the grandeur of our people, the grandeur of our homeland, that beauty, that sweet hope for our homeland, which we must reach.

CHAPTER SIX

Questions and Answers

In this chapter, we will listen to words spoken by Pope Francis on a number of different occasions when he met young people and answered their questions. The Pope's responses are grouped under a number of headings. What's clear from the way the Pope responds to the questions is that he doesn't have a set of prepared answers. He really engages with the person asking the question. The topics range from the nature of love to how to overcome darkness and fears that many young people experience, to how to really live a life that leaves a mark on history.

It is striking to hear Pope Francis speak of the challenge that tragedies in our world put before us. How many today feel there is a 'silence of God'. Pope Francis doesn't talk as if he were someone immune from those challenges. But, walking along side us, he offers the wisdom he has distilled through his own life experience and reflection.

The Pope also encourages young people to be pro-active in life, taking on permanent commitments, whether it be in marriage, priesthood or religious life. And, also to be pro-active in transforming our world, or some other form of committed service to humankind, not letting themselves be trapped by harmful aspects of some media, peer pressure or corruption, but rather tackling issues of poverty, injustice, destruction of human dignity.

Above all, Pope Francis' answers are seasoned with an invitation to see things through the eyes of faith and love that we find in God. With God, everything is possible and so we don't have to be robbed of hope.

How Can We Experience Jesus' Love?

At a youth gathering in Turin a girl called Chiara asked Pope Francis the following question: 'Often we feel disappointed in love. What does the greatness of Jesus' love consist in? How can we experience his love?'[5]

> You know that it is awful to see a young person 'standing still'. He or she is alive but living – allow me use the word – like a vegetable: he or she does things, but their life is not a life that moves, it stands still. But you know that it makes me very sad at heart to see young people retire at twenty! Yes, they age quickly … Therefore, when Chiara asked that question on love: what keeps a young person from retiring is the desire to love, the desire to give what is most beautiful of human beings, and what is most beautiful of God, because the definition that John gives of God is 'God is love'. And when a young person loves, lives, grows, he or she does not retire. He or she grows, grows, grows and gives.

But what is love? 'Is it a soap opera, Father? What we see on TV programmes?' Some think that that is love. It is so good to speak of love, very beautiful, beautiful, beautiful things can be said. However, love has two axles on which it revolves, and if a person, a young person doesn't have these two axles – these two dimensions of love – it's not love. First of all, *love is more in works than in words: love is concrete* ... Love is concrete, it is more in deeds than in words. It's not love to just say: 'I love you, I love all people'. No. What do you do for love? Love gives itself. Consider that God began to speak of love when He engaged his people, when He chose his people, He made a covenant with his people, He saved his people, He forgave so many times – God has so much patience! – He did (things), He performed gestures of love, works of love.

And the second dimension, the second axle on which love revolves is that *love is always communicated*, that is, love listens and responds, *love is built in dialogue, in communion*: it is communicated. Love is neither deaf nor mute, it communicates. These two dimensions are very useful to understand what love is, which is not a romantic sentiment of the moment or a story. No. It's concrete, it's in deeds. And it is communicated, that is, it is always in dialogue.

So Chiara, I will answer your question: 'Often we feel disappointed in love. What does the greatness of Jesus' love consist in? How can we experience his love?' And now, I know that you are good and will permit me to speak sincerely. I don't want to be a moralist but I would like to say a word that isn't liked, an unpopular word. Sometimes the Pope must also take risks to speak the truth. Love is in works, in communicating, but love is very respectful of people, it does not use people, that is, *love is chaste*. And to you young people in this world, in this hedonistic world, in this world where only pleasure, having a good time, and living the good life get publicity, I say to you: be chaste, be chaste.

All of us in life have gone through moments in which this virtue has been very difficult, but it is in fact the way of genuine love, of a love that is able to give life, which does not seek to use the other for one's own pleasure. It is a love that considers the life of the other person sacred: 'I respect you, I don't want to use you, I don't want to use you'. It's not easy. We all know the difficulties in overcoming the 'care-free' and hedonistic conception of love. Forgive me if I say something you weren't expecting, but I ask you: strive to experience love chastely.

And from this we draw a conclusion: if love is respectful, if love is in deeds, if love is in communicating, *love makes sacrifices for others*. Look at the love of parents, of so many mothers, of so many fathers who in the morning arrive at work tired because they haven't slept well in order to look after their sick child – this is love! This is respect. This is not having a good time. This is – let's go to another key word – this is *'service'*. *Love is service*. It is serving others. When, after the washing of the feet, Jesus explained the gesture to the Apostles, he taught that we are made to serve one another, and if I say that I love but I don't serve the other, don't help the other, don't enable him to go forward, don't sacrifice myself for him, this isn't love. You have carried the Cross*: there is the sign of love. That history of God's love involved in works and

---

* The World Youth Day Cross is carried around the world to different places in between the main World Youth Day event held every two or three years.

dialogue, with respect, with forgiveness, with patience during so many centuries of history with his people, ends there – his Son on the Cross, the greatest service, which is giving one's life, sacrificing oneself, helping others. It's not easy to speak of love, it's not easy to experience love. However, with these things that I have said, Chiara, I think I've helped you with something, with the questions you asked me. I don't know, I hope they will be beneficial to you.

What is Real Love? Don't be Afraid of Surprises!

During his 2015 trip to the Philippines, Pope Francis met young people at the Sports field of Santo Tomás University, Manila. In the course of the gathering, various young people spoke, including a young man, Leandro Santos, who asked about information and technology. In his impromptu speech in reply to these questions, Pope Francis spoke about the risk of information overload today. We have plenty of information, he said, but maybe we don't know what to do with it all. We risk becoming 'museums', storing up all sorts of things but not knowing what to do with them. Pope Francis remarked that there's a need for young people today who not only have plenty of information but who are also wise. He then continued his speech as follows …

You can ask me: Father, how can I become wise? This is another challenge: the challenge of love. What is the most important lesson which you have to learn at the University? What is the most important lesson that you have to learn in life? It is learning how to love. This is the challenge which life sets before you today. Learning how to love. Not just how to accumulate information. There comes a time when you don't know what to do with it all. It's a storehouse. Unless, through love, all this information can bear fruit.

For this to happen, the Gospel proposes to us a serene and tranquil thing to do. It is to use three languages: the language of the mind, the language of the heart and the language of the hands. All three together, harmoniously: what you think, you feel and you do. Your information descends to the heart, moves it and gets translated into action. And all this in a harmonious way: I think what I feel and do, I feel what I think and what I do, and I do what I think and what I feel. The three languages ... Thinking, feeling and acting.[6]

True love is both loving and letting oneself be loved. It is harder to let ourselves be loved than it is to love. That is why it is so hard to achieve the perfect love of God, because we can love him but the important thing is to let ourselves be loved by him. Real love is being open to that love which was there first and catches us by surprise. If all you have is information, you are closed to surprises. Love makes you open to surprises. Love is always a surprise, because it starts with a dialogue between two persons: the one who loves and the one who is loved.

We say that God is the God of surprises, because he always loved us first and he waits to take us by surprise. God surprises us. Let's allow ourselves to be surprised by God. Let's not have the psychology of a computer, thinking that we know everything. What do I mean? Think for a moment: the computer has all the answers: never a surprise. In the challenge of love, God shows up with surprises.

Think of Saint Matthew. He was a good businessman. He also betrayed his country because he collected taxes from the Jews and paid them to the Romans. He was loaded with money and he collected taxes. Then Jesus comes along, looks at him and says: 'Come, follow me'. Matthew couldn't believe it. If you have some time later, go look at the picture that Caravaggio painted about this scene. Jesus called him, like this (*stretching out his hand*). Those who were with Jesus were saying: '[He is calling] this man, a traitor, a scoundrel?' And

Matthew hangs on to his money and doesn't want to leave. But the surprise of being loved wins him over and he follows Jesus. That morning, when Matthew was going off to work and said goodbye to his wife, he never thought that he was going to return in a hurry, without money to tell his wife to prepare a banquet. The banquet for the one who loved him first, who surprised him with something important, more important than all the money he had.

So let yourselves be surprised by God! Don't be afraid of surprises, afraid that they will shake you up. They make us insecure, but they change the direction we are going in. Real love makes you 'burn life', even at the risk of coming up empty-handed. Think of Saint Francis: he left everything, he died with empty hands, but with a full heart.

Do you agree? Not young people who are 'museums', 'storehouses', but young people who are wise. To be wise, use the three languages: think well, feel well and act well. And to be wise, let yourselves be surprised by God's love, then go out and burn life!

How Do You Overcome the Negative Experience of Being Abandoned?

During a meeting with young people during his visit in 2015 to Kenya, Uganda and the Central African Republic, the issue came up of those who have not experienced love in their lives. The question was asked: 'What do you have to say to those young people who have not experienced love in their own families? How can they move beyond this?'[7]

Everywhere there are young people who were abandoned, either at birth or later on, by their family, their parents, and so they have never known the love of a family. That is why families are so important. Protect the family! Defend it always. All around us, there are not only abandoned children, but also abandoned elderly persons, who have no one to visit them, to show them affection ... How do you overcome this negative experience of being abandoned, of not being loved? There is only one remedy: to give what you have not received. If you have not received understanding, then show understanding to others. If you have not received love, then show love to others. If you have known loneliness, then try to be close to others who are lonely. Flesh is cured with flesh! And God took flesh in order to heal us. So let us do the same with others.

On Doubt and Difficulties

At a Turin meeting of young people a girl called Sara asked Pope Francis the following question:[8] 'I think of Jesus' words, "Give your life". Often we have a sense of doubt in life. But, is it worthwhile to live like this? What can I expect from this life?'

Thank you, Sara. Let's consider the wars in the world. A few times I have said that we are experiencing the Third World War, but piecemeal. Piecemeal: there is war in Europe, there is war in Africa, there is war in the Middle East, there is war in other countries ... But, can I have confidence in such a life? Can I trust world leaders? When I go to vote for a candidate, can I trust that he won't lead my country into war? If you only trust in humankind, you have lost!

It makes me think one thing: people, leaders, entrepreneurs who call themselves Christians, and manufacture arms! This gives rise to some mistrust: they call themselves Christians! 'No, no, Father, I don't manufacture them, no, no ... I only have my savings, my investments in arms factories.' Ah! And why? 'Because the interest is somewhat higher ...'

And being two-faced is common currency today: saying one thing and doing another. Hypocrisy ... But we see what happened in the last century: in 1914, 1915... There was that great tragedy in Armenia. So many died. I don't know the figure: more than a million certainly. But where were the great powers of the time? They were looking the other way. Why? Because they were interested in war: their war! And those who died were people, second-class human beings.

Then, in the 1930s and 1940s the tragedy of the Shoah. The great powers had photographs of the railroads that took trains to the concentration camps, such as Auschwitz, to kill Jews, and also Christians, also homosexuals, to kill them there. But tell me, why didn't they bomb that? Interest! And shortly after, almost contemporaneously, there was the Russian Gulag, under Stalin ... How many Christians suffered, were killed! The great powers divided Europe among themselves like a cake. So many years had to pass before reaching a 'certain' freedom. There is that hypocrisy of speaking of peace and producing arms, and even selling arms to this one who is at war with that one, and to that one who is at war with this one!

I understand what you are saying about doubts in life; today too, when we are living in the throw-away culture. Because whatever is not economically useful is thrown away. Children are thrown away, because they are not conceived or because they are killed before they are born; the elderly are thrown away, because they are not needed or are left there, to die, a sort of hidden euthanasia, and we don't help them to live; and now young people are discarded: think of that 40 per cent of young people who are without work. It is in fact a waste! But why? In the global economic system, the god of money is at the centre instead of man and woman, as God wants. Everything is done for money.

In Spanish, there is a good saying ... 'Por la plata baila el mono'. I will translate: Even the monkey dances for money. And so, with this throw-away culture, with this growing sense of challenge can one trust life? A young person who can't study, who doesn't have a job, who has the shame of not feeling worthy because he or she doesn't have work, is not earning a living … But how many times do these young people end up with addictions! How often they commit suicide? The statistics on suicide among young people are not well known. Or how often these young people go to fight with terrorists, at least to do something, for an ideal. I understand this challenge. And this is why Jesus told us not to place our security in riches, in worldly powers. How can I trust life? What can I do, how can I live a life that doesn't destroy, that isn't a life of destruction, a life that doesn't throw people away? How can I live a life that doesn't disappoint me?…

We must go ahead with our plans for building [a project for sharing]. Such a life does not disappoint. If you get involved in a plan for building, [sharing], helping – let's think of street children, of migrants, of so many in need, but not only to feed them for one day, two days, but to work for their development through education, with unity in the joy of the Oratories [local parish initiatives] … then that sense of mistrust in life recedes, it goes away.

What must I do (to achieve this)? Don't retire too early. Do something! And I'll say another thing: go against the tide. Go against the tide. For you who are young, you who are living this economic situation, which is also cultural, hedonistic, consumerist, with values like 'soap bubbles', there is no moving forward with such values. Do constructive things, even if small, but which unite us, which bring us together with our ideals: this is the best antidote against a mistrust of life, against a culture that only offers you pleasure: to have a good time, to have money and not think about other things.

So often advertisements try to convince us that this is good, that that is good, and they lead us to believe that they are 'diamonds'; but be careful, they are selling glass! And we must go against this, not being naïve. Not buying filth that they tell us are diamonds.

And, in conclusion, I would like to repeat the words of Pier Giorgio Frassati: if you want to do something good in life, *live, don't just get by*. Live! But you are intelligent and surely you will tell me: 'But, Father, you speak this way because you are in the Vatican, you have so many monsignors there who do the work, you are at ease and don't know what everyday life is...' Yes, one could think so. The secret is to understand clearly where one lives ... At the end of the nineteenth century, the conditions for young people's development (in this area of Turin) were the worst possible. Freemasonry was in full swing, not even the Church could do anything. There were priest haters, there were also Satanists ... It was one of the worst moments and one of the worst places in the history of Italy. However, if you would like to do a nice homework assignment, go and find out how many men and women saints were born during that time. Why? Because they realised that they had to go against the tide with respect to the culture, to that lifestyle. Reality, live the reality. And if this reality is glass and not diamonds, I search for the reality against the tide and I create my reality, but something that is of service to others. Think of your saints of this land, what they did!

Always love and life, friends. However, these words can only be lived by 'going forth': always going forth to contribute to something. If you stand still, you won't do anything in life and you will ruin your own.

Do Not be Afraid of Failure!

At a meeting in the Vatican between Pope Francis and Jesuit students of Italy and Albania, one of the young people spoke to Pope Francis of his search and doubts linked to adolescence.[9] 'As I wrote in my letter to you I am searching ... However I have difficulties. Sometimes I have doubts. And I believe that this is absolutely normal for my age. Since you are the Pope who I believe I will have the longest in my heart, in my life, because I am meeting you in the time of my adolescence, of my development, I want to ask you for a few words to help me in my growth and to support all other young people like me.'

Walking is an art; if we are always in a hurry we tire and cannot reach our destination, the destination of our journey. Yet if we stop and do not move, we also fail to reach our destination. Walking is precisely the art of looking to the horizon, thinking about where I want to go, and also coping with the weariness that comes from walking. Moreover, the way is often hard-going, it is not easy ... There are days of darkness, days of failure, and some days of falling ... Yet always keep this in your thoughts: do not be afraid of failure, do not be afraid of falling. In the art of walking it is not falling that matters, but rather 'staying fallen'. Get up quickly, immediately, and continue to go on. And this is beautiful: it is working every day, it is walking humanly. But also, it is terrible to walk alone, terrible and tedious. Walking in community, with friends, with those who love us: this helps us, it helps us to arrive precisely at the destination where we must arrive. I don't know if I have answered your question. Have you understood? You won't be afraid of the journey? Thank you.

How Can we See God's Hand in the Tragedies of Life?

During a meeting with young people during his visit in 2015 to Kenya, Uganda and the Central African Republic, guests asked Pope Francis many questions about the difficulties they were facing – divisions, fighting, wars, death, fanaticism, tribalism, corruption: 'How can we realise that God is our Father? How can we see God's hand in the tragedies of life? How we find God's peace?'

This question is asked by men and women the world over in one way or another. And they don't come up with an answer. There are some questions to which, no matter how hard we try, we never seem to find an answer. 'How can I see the hand of God in one of life's tragedies?' There is only one answer: no, there is no answer. There is only a way: to look to the Son of God. God delivered his Son to save us all. God let himself get hurt. God let himself be destroyed on the cross. So when the moment comes when you don't understand, when you're in despair and the world is tumbling down all around you, look to the cross! There we see the failure of God; there we see the destruction of God. But there we also see a challenge to our faith: the challenge of hope. Because that story didn't end in failure. There was the Resurrection, which made all things new.

I'll tell you a secret. In my pocket I always carry two things: a Rosary, to pray, and something else which may seem a little odd ... What is it? It's the story of God's failure: it is a little Way of the Cross, the story of how Jesus suffered from the time he was condemned to death until his burial. With these two things, I try to do my best. But thanks to these two things I don't lose hope.

On the Silence of God

In Naples a young girl named Bianca asked Pope Francis the following question:[10] 'You teach us that apostles must push themselves to be courteous, calm, enthusiastic and happy people, individuals who spread joy wherever they go. This is very true for us! And yet, our hearts really yearn to hope and dream. It then often becomes difficult to reconcile our Christian values with the horrors, difficulties and corruption which surround us every day. Holy Father, amid the "silence of God" how can we sow seeds of joy and hope so that the land bears the fruit of authenticity and truth, justice and real love that goes beyond every human limitation?'

God, our God, is a God of words. He is a God of gestures. He is a God of silences. We know He is a God of words because God's words are in the Bible: God speaks to us, He looks for us. The God of gestures is the God who goes out. Let us think of the Parable of the Good Shepherd who goes out to look for us, who calls us by name, who knows us better than we know ourselves, who is always waiting for us, who always forgives us, who always communicates his understanding to us through gestures of tenderness.

And then there is the God of silence. Think of the great moments of silence in the Bible: for example, Abraham's silent heart when he went with his son to offer him in sacrifice. He went up the mountain for two days and didn't dare say anything to his son, though the son was not foolish, he understood. God was silent. But the greatest silence of God was on the Cross: Jesus felt the Father's silence, calling it 'abandonment'. 'Father, why have you abandoned me? And then there was the miracle of God, that word, that magnificent gesture which was the Resurrection.

Our God is also a God of silences and there are silences of God which cannot be explained until you look at the Crucifixion. For example, why do children suffer? Can you explain that to me? Where can you find the words of God to explain the suffering of children? This is one of those great silences of God. I am not saying that we can 'understand' the silences of God, but we can come close to them by looking at Christ crucified, Christ who died, Christ abandoned, from the Mount of Olives to the Cross. These are the moments of silence.

'But God created us to be happy' – 'Yes, it's true'. But He is often silent. And this is also true. I cannot deceive you by saying: 'No, have faith and everything will be ok, you will be happy, you will have good luck, you will have money …' No, our God is silent. Remember: He is the God of words, the God of gestures and the God of silences. You must bring these three things together in your life. This is what comes to my mind to tell you. I am sorry, I don't have any other 'recipe'.

Television and Social Media

During a question and answer session with young people in Sarajevo, Pope Francis was asked about the fact that he had stopped watching television. He responded as follows.[11]

Yes, from the mid-1990s onwards, I felt one night that watching television was not good for me, it distanced me, and led me away… and I decided not to watch anymore. When I wanted to see a good film, I went to the television room in the Archbishop's residence and watched it there. But just that film. The television used to make me feel alienated from myself. And yes, I am from the Stone Age, I am ancient!

I understand that the times have changed; we live in an age of images. And this is very important. In an age of images we must do what was done in the age of books: choose what is good for me! Out of this come two consequences: the responsibility of television networks to offer programmes, which encourage the good, which promote values, which build up society, which help us advance, not ones that drag us down. And then to produce programmes that help us so that values, true values, may be reinforced and may help to prepare us for life. This is the responsibility of television networks.

Secondly, knowing how to choose what programs to watch, and this is our responsibility. If I watch a program that is not good for me, that disparages my values, that leads me to become vulgar, even filthy, I need to change the channel. As was done in my Stone Age: when a book was good, you read it; when a book was not good for you, you would throw it away.

And this leads to a third point: the point of evil fantasy, of those fantasies which kill the soul. If you who are young live attached to your computers and become slaves to the computer, you lose your freedom! And if you use your computer to look for dirty programs, you lose your dignity.

Watch television, use the computer, but for beautiful reasons, for great things, things which help us to grow. This is good.

Today, with so many kinds of media, we are informed, even over-informed. Is this a bad thing? No. It is good and useful, but we do run the risk of information overload. We have plenty of information, but maybe we don't know what to do with it all. We risk becoming 'museums', storing up all sorts of things but not knowing what to do with them. We don't need young people who are storehouses, but young people who are wise.[12]

Young People and Marriage

During a trip to Assisi, Pope Francis met with young people from the region of Umbria in Italy. The question of marriage came up and a couple asked the following:[13] 'We young people live in a society where feeling good, having fun and thinking of oneself is central. Living married life as young Christians is complex, and being open to life is often challenging and frightening. As a young couple, we feel the joy of living out our marriage, but we also experience its daily struggles and challenges. How can the Church help us, how can our pastors support us, and what steps are we called to make?'

I am glad that *the first question* came from a young married couple. What a beautiful witness! Two young people who have chosen, who have joyfully and courageously decided to form a family. Yes, it is so true that it takes courage to form a family. It takes courage! And your question, young spouses, is linked to *the question of vocation*. What is marriage? It is a *true and authentic vocation*, as are the priesthood and the religious life. Two Christians who marry have recognised the call of the Lord in their own love story, the vocation to form one flesh and one life from two, male and female. And the Sacrament of Holy Matrimony envelops this love in the grace of God, it roots it in God himself. By this gift, and by the certainty of this call, you can continue on assured; you have nothing to fear; you can face everything together!

Let us think about our parents, about our grandparents and great grandparents. They married in much poorer conditions than our own. Some married during wartime or just after a war. Some like my own parents emigrated. Where did they find the strength? They found it in the certainty that the Lord was with them, that their families were blessed by God through the Sacrament of Matrimony, and that the mission of bringing children into the world and educating them is also blessed. With this assurance they overcame even the most difficult trials. These were simple certainties, but they were real; they were the pillars that supported their love. Their lives were not easy; there were problems, many, many problems. However, these simple assurances helped them to go forward. And they succeeded in having beautiful families, and in giving life and in raising their children.

Dear friends, this moral and spiritual foundation is necessary in order to build well in a lasting way! Today, this foundation is no longer guaranteed by family life and the social tradition. Indeed, the society in which you were raised favours individual rights rather than the families: these individual rights. It favours relationships that last until difficulties arise, and this is why it sometimes speaks about relationships between couples, within families and between spouses in a superficial and misleading way. It is enough to watch certain television programmes to see these values on display!

How many times parish priests – sometimes I myself also heard it – hear a couple that comes to get married say: 'But you both know that marriage is for life?' 'Ah, we love each other so much, but … we'll stay together as long as the love lasts. When it ends, we'll each go our separate way.' This is selfishness: when I feel like it, I'll end the marriage and forget the 'one flesh' that cannot be separated. It is risky to get married: it is risky! It is this selfishness which threatens it, because we each have within us this possibility of a dual personality: the one that says, 'I am free, I want this …' and the other which says, 'I, me, to me, with me, for me …' Selfishness always returns and does not know how to open up to others.

The other difficulty is this culture of the temporary: it seems as though nothing is definitive. Everything is provisional. As I said before: love, as long as it lasts. I once heard a seminarian – a good person – say: 'I want to become a priest, but for ten years. Then I'll rethink it.' This is the culture of the temporary, and Jesus didn't save us temporarily: he saved us definitively!

However, the Holy Spirit is always stirring up new answers to new needs! Thus, programs for engaged couples, marriage preparation courses, parish groups for young couples and family movements have been multiplying in the Church. They are an immense wealth! They are reference points for everyone: young people searching, couples in crisis, parents having difficulties with their children or vice versa. They help everyone!

And so I wish to tell you *not to be afraid to take definitive steps*: do not be afraid to take them. How many times I have heard mothers tell me: 'But, Father, I have a son who is thirty years old and he won't get married. I don't know what to do! He has a beautiful girlfriend, but he won't make up his mind.' Well, Madame, stop ironing his shirts! That's how it is! Do not be afraid to take steps which are permanent, like getting married: deepen your love by respecting its seasons and expressions, pray, prepare yourselves well; and then trust that the Lord will not leave you alone! Let him come into your home like one of the family, He will always support you!

How Do we Recognise God is Calling Us?

Continuing his conversation with young people in Assisi during his visit there, Pope Francis responded to a question on the theme of vocation.[14] 'What should I do with my life? How and where should I invest the talents which the Lord has given me? Sometimes the idea of the priesthood or consecrated life attracts me, but then fear immediately arises. And then, such a commitment 'forever'? How do we recognise God's call? What counsel would you give to someone who wants to dedicate their life to the service of God and their brothers and sisters?'

Family life is the vocation that God inscribed into the nature of man and woman and there is another vocation which is complementary to marriage: *the call to celibacy and virginity for the sake of the Kingdom of Heaven*. It is the vocation that Jesus himself lived. How do you recognise it? How do you follow it? I will respond with two essential elements on how to recognise the vocation to the priesthood and to consecrated life. *Praying and walking in the Church*. These two go together, they are intertwined.

A powerful experience of God is always at the origin of every vocation to consecrated life, an unforgettable experience that you remember for the rest of your life! This is what happened to Francis. And this is not something we can calculate or plan. God always surprises us! It is God who calls; however, it is important to have a daily relationship with him, to listen to him in silence before the Tabernacle and deep within ourselves, to speak with him, to draw near to the sacraments. Having this familiar relationship with the Lord is like keeping the window of our lives open so that he can make us hear his voice and hear what he wants us to do.

It would be beautiful to hear from you, to hear from the priests who are present, from the sisters … It would be very beautiful, because each story is unique. However, they all begin with an encounter that illumines you deeply within, that touches the heart and engages the whole person: affections, intellect, senses, everything.

A relationship with God does not only involve one part of us, it involves everything. It is a love so great, so beautiful, so true, that it deserves everything, and it deserves all our trust. And there is one thing I would like to tell you forcefully, especially today: virginity for the Kingdom of God is not a 'no', it is a 'yes'! Of course it involves the renunciation of the marriage bond and of having a family of one's own, but at its foundation and core there is a 'yes', as a response to Christ's total 'yes' to us, and this 'yes' makes us fruitful.

With the Lord Everything is Possible

A teenager attending a Jesuit school met with Pope Francis in the Vatican during an audience of Jesuit students. I would like to ask you a quick question. 'How did you get through it when you decided to become, not Pope, but a parish priest, a Jesuit? How did you do it? Wasn't it difficult for you to abandon or leave your family and friends?'[15]

You know, it is always difficult. Always. It was hard for me. It is far from easy. There are beautiful moments, and Jesus helps you, he gives you a little joy. All the same there are difficult moments when you feel alone, when you feel dry, without any interior joy. There are clouded moments of interior darkness. There are hardships. But it is so beautiful to follow Jesus, to walk in the footsteps of Jesus, that you then find balance and move forward. And then come even more wonderful moments. But no one must think that there will not be difficult moments in life … How do you think you can move forward with hardships? It isn't easy; but we must go ahead with strength and with trust in the Lord, with the Lord everything is possible.

Transform the World

During a meeting with young people of Umbria in Assisi, a young person, looking to the future, asked Pope Francis for advice on how to transform our world.[16] 'How should a young Christian look to the future? Which roads should he take toward building a society worthy of God and worthy of man?'

The Gospel is not only about religion. It about humanity, the whole of humanity. The Gospel is about the world, society and human civilization. The Gospel is God's message of salvation for humankind. When we say 'message of salvation', this is not simply a way of speaking, these are not mere words or empty words like so many today. Humankind truly needs to be saved! We see it everyday when we flip through newspapers or watch the news on television; but we also see it around us, in people, in situations; and we see it in ourselves! Each one of us needs to be saved! We cannot do it alone! We need to be saved!

Saved from what? From evil. Evil is at work, it does its job. However, evil is not invincible and a Christian does not give up when confronted by evil. And you who are young people, do you want to give up in the face of evil, injustice and difficulty? [Young people reply: No!] Ah, good. I like this. Our secret is that God is greater than evil: this is true! God is greater than evil. God is infinite love, boundless mercy, and that Love has conquered evil at its root through the death and Resurrection of Christ. This is the Gospel, the Good News: God's love has won! Christ died on the cross for our sins and rose again. With him we can fight evil and conquer every day. Do we believe this or not? [Young people respond: Yes!] But that 'yes' has to become part of life! If I believe that Jesus has conquered evil and saved me, I must follow along the path of Jesus for my whole life.

The Gospel, then, this message of salvation, has two destinations that are connected: the first, to awaken faith, and this is evangelisation; the second, to transform the world according to God's plan, and this is the Christian animation of society. But these are not two separate things, they form one mission: to carry the Gospel by the witness of our lives in order to transform the world! This is the way: to bring the Gospel by the witness of our lives.

Let us look to [St] Francis: he did both of these things, through the power of the one Gospel. Francis made faith grow and he renewed the Church, and at the same time he renewed society, he made it more fraternal, but he always did it with the Gospel and by his witness. Do you know what Francis once said to his brothers? He said: 'Always preach the Gospel and if necessary use words!' But how? Is it possible to preach the Gospel without words? Yes! By your witness! First comes witness, then come words!

Young people of Umbria: you must also do something! Today, in the name of St Francis, I say to you: I have neither gold nor silver to give you, but something far more precious, the Gospel of Jesus. Go forward with courage! With the Gospel in heart and hands, be witnesses of faith by your lives: bring Christ into your home, preach him among your friends, welcome and serve him in the poor. Young people, give Umbria a message of life, peace and hope! You can do it!

Crisis is Not a Bad Thing

During the meeting with Jesuit students of Italy and Albania, a young woman asked Pope Francis for some direction given the difficult situation her country was in. 'I would like to ask you for a word about today's youth, about the future of young people today, considering the difficult situation that Italy is in. And I would like to ask for your help in improving that situation, help for us, so that we young people can move ahead.'

You say that Italy is going through a difficult time. Yes, there is a crisis. But I will tell you this: it is not only in Italy. Right now the whole world is in crisis. And crisis is not a bad thing. It is true that the crisis causes us suffering but we – and first and foremost all you young people – must know how to interpret the crisis.

What does this crisis mean? What must I do to help us to come through this crisis? The crisis we are experiencing at this time is a human crisis. People say: it is an economic crisis, it is a crisis of work. Yes, that's true. But why? This work problem, this problem in the economy, is a consequence of the great human problem. What is in crisis is the value of the human person, and we must defend the human person.

I once read a story about a medieval rabbi in the year 1200. This rabbi explained to the Jews of that time the history of the Tower of Babel. Building the Tower of Babel was not easy. They had to make bricks; and how is a brick made? Mud and straw must be fetched, they must be mixed and the bricks brought to the kiln. It involved a lot of work. And after all this work a brick became a real treasure! They then had to hoist the bricks in order to build the Tower of Babel. If a brick fell it was a tragedy!

But if a man fell nothing happened! It is this crisis that we are living today, this same crisis. It is the crisis of the person.

Today the person counts for nothing; it is coins, it is money that counts. And Jesus, God, gave the world, the whole creation, to the person, to men and women that they might care for it; he did not give it to money. It is a crisis, the person is in a crisis because today the person is a slave! We must liberate ourselves from these economic and social structures that enslave us. This is your duty.

A Corrupt Person is Not at Peace

During his meeting with young people on his visit to Kenya, Uganda and the Central African Republic in 2015, the issue of corruption arose. How best can it be tackled? 'Can corruption be justified simply because everyone is involved in wrongdoing, everyone is corrupt? How can we be Christians and fight the evil of corruption?'[17]

I remember, in my own country, a young person, about twenty years old, who wanted to get involved in politics. He studied, he was enthusiastic … and he got a job in a government office. One day he had to make a decision about purchasing something. He had three estimates, so he reviewed them and he chose the best one. Then he went to his boss to have it approved. 'Why did you choose this one?' 'Because it was best for the country's finances'. 'No, no, you have to choose the one which will put more money in your pocket!' This young person told his boss: 'I got into politics to help my country!', and the boss's answer was, 'I got into politics to steal!' This is just one example. There is corruption not just in politics but in every institution, even in the Vatican. Corruption is something which creeps in. It's like sugar: it's sweet, we like it, it goes down easily. And then? We get sick! We come to a nasty end! With all that easy sugar we end up as diabetics, and our country becomes diabetic!

Whenever we take a bribe, or pocket a kickback, we destroy our heart, we destroy our personality, we destroy our country. Please, don't get used to the taste of this 'sugar' which is corruption. 'But Father, I see corruption everywhere, I see so many people selling themselves for a handful of money without any concern for the lives of others …' As in everything, you have to make a start. If in your heart you don't like corruption, if you do not want corruption in your life in your country, then start now! If you don't start, your neighbour won't start either. Corruption also steals our joy. It robs us of peace. A corrupt person is not at peace.

Once in my city – this is a true story – a man died. Everybody knew he was a big crook. A few days later, I asked what the funeral was like. One lady who had a good sense of humour told me: 'Father, they couldn't even close the coffin, because he tried to bring with him all the money he had stolen!' Whatever you steal by corruption will stay behind and somebody else will use it. But it will also stay behind – and we need to keep this in mind – in the hearts of all those men and women who were hurt by your example of corruption. It will stay behind in all the good you could have done but never did. It will stay behind in the children who are sick or hungry because the money that was meant for them was used for your own enjoyment, because you were corrupt. Dear young people, corruption is not the way to life. It is a path which leads to death.

Poverty

During a meeting with Jesuit students of Italy and Albania, a young man brought up the topic of poverty, a topic that Pope Francis has often spoken about: 'As you well know from your experience, we have learned to experience and coexist with many different kinds of poverty … material poverty, spiritual poverty … I would like to ask you: how can we young people live with this poverty? How should we behave?'[18]

First of all I would like to say one thing to all of you: do not let yourselves be robbed of hope! Please, do not let yourselves be robbed of it! And who robs you of hope? The spirit of the world, wealth, the spirit of vanity, arrogance, pride. All these things steal hope from you.

Where do I find hope? In the poor Jesus, Jesus who made himself poor for us. And you mentioned poverty. Poverty demands that we sow hope. It requires me too to have greater hope. This seems a little hard to understand, but I remember that Fr Arrupe [a former Jesuit Superior General] once wrote a good letter to the [Jesuit] Centres for Social Research … He spoke of how the social problem must be studied. But in the end he told us, he said to all of us: 'Look, it is impossible to talk about poverty without having an experience with the poor'… It is impossible to talk about poverty, about abstract poverty. That does not exist!

Poverty is the flesh of the poor Jesus in this hungry child, in the sick person, in these unjust social structures. Go, look over there at the flesh of Jesus. But do not let yourselves be robbed of hope by prosperity, by the spirit of prosperity which, in the end brings you to become a nothing in life! The young must stake themselves on high ideals: this is my advice. But where do I find hope? In the flesh of the suffering Jesus and in true poverty. There is a connection between the two.

Endnotes

1. Pope Francis, Address at the Welcoming Ceremony at World Youth Day, Jordan Park, Błonia, Kraków, Thursday, 28 July 2016.

2. Way of Cross Ceremony, Jordan Park in Błonia, Kraków, Friday, 29 July 2016.

3. Pope Francis, Address at the Prayer Vigil with Young People, Campus Misericordiae, Kraków, Saturday, 30 July 2016.

4. Pope Francis' words during the Meeting with Young People at the Fr Félix Varela Cultural Center, Havana, Sunday, 20 September 2015.

5. Address to Children and Young People in Piazzo Vittorio, Turin, Sunday, 21 June 2015.

6. Philippines, 18 January 2015.

7. Meeting with Young People at the Kasarani Stadium, Nairobi (Kenya), 27 November 2015.

8. Address to Children and Young People in Piazzo Vittorio, Turin.

9. See Pope Francis, Conversation in the Vatican with Jesuit students of Italy and Albania, 7 June 2013.

10. Meeting with Young People, Naples, Saturday, 21 March 2015; Sunday, 21 June 2015.

11. Meeting with Young People at the John Paul II Diocesan Youth Centre in Sarajevo, Saturday, 6 June 2015.

12. Philippines, 18 January 2015.

13. Meeting with Young People of Umbria in the square in front of the Basilica of Saint Mary of the Angels, Assisi, Friday, 4 October 2013.

14. Meeting with Young People of Umbria in the square in front of the Basilica of Saint Mary of the Angels, Assisi, Friday, 4 October 2013.

15. A conversation in the Vatican with Jesuit students of Italy and Albania, 7 June 2013.

16. Meeting with Young People of Umbria in the square in front of the Basilica of Saint Mary of the Angels, Assisi, Friday, 4 October 2013.

17. Meeting with Young People at the Kasarani Stadium, Nairobi (Kenya), 27 November 2015.

18. Pope Francis, Conversation with the Jesuit Students of Italy and Albania, 7 June 2013.